Bob Artley's
Book of
Farm Chores

As Remembered by a Former Kid

By Bob Artley

Paul Gruchow, Editor

Voyageur Press

Edited by Paul Gruchow
Cover Design by JoDee Turner
Printed in China

02   03   04   05   06   5   4   3   2   1

Library of Congress Cataloging-in-Publication Data
Artley, Bob.
    Bob Artley's book of farm chores : as remembered by a former kid / by Bob Artley ; edited by Paul Gruchow.
        p. cm.
    ISBN 0-89658-434-8 (pbk. : alk. paper)
    1. Farm life—Iowa. 2. Farm life—Iowa—Caricatures and cartoons. 3. Iowa—Social life and customs.
4. Iowa—Social life and customs—Caricatures and cartoons. 5. American wit and humor, Pictorial. 6.
Artley, Bob—Childhood and youth. 7. Iowa—Biography. I. Title: Book of farm chores. II. Title.
    F621 .A75 2002
    977.7'033—dc21
                        2002004667

Distributed in Canada by Raincoast Books
9050 Shaughnessy Street, Vancouver, B.C. V6P 6E5

Published by Voyageur Press, Inc.
123 North Second Street, P.O. Box 338, Stillwater, MN 55082 U.S.A.
651-430-2210, fax 651-430-2211
books@voyageurpress.com
www.voyageurpress.com

Educators, fundraisers, premium and gift buyers, publicists, and marketing managers: Looking for creative products and new sales ideas? Voyageur Press books are available at special discounts when purchased in quantities, and special editions can be created to your specifications. For details contact the marketing department at 800-888-9653.

This book is dedicated to my grandchildren,
that they might know what they have missed.

Contents

Acknowledgments, **5**

To begin with, **6**

First came the chickens, **10**

Coping with pigs, **18**

Our great and gentle beasts, **24**

Cattle call, **36**

The education of a milker, **46**

Housecleaning and other calamities, **64**

Chores on ice, **88**

Acknowledgments

The drawings in this book first appeared in a cartoon series in the *Worthington Daily Globe* in 1983 and 1984 under the title "Chores, as we remember them."

Except for a portion of Chapter 8, "Chores on ice," that first appeared as a story in a February 1979 issue of the *Globe* under the title "Winter Chores," the text was all written expressly for this book. The illustration on the cover is from a watercolor painting accompanying that story.

My thanks to Paul Gruchow, former *Daily Globe* managing editor with whom I worked for several delightful years, for his inspiring and professional guidance in the preparation and editing of this book.

Chapter 1
To Begin with . . .

I must have been in college before I realized that the word "chores" referred to tasks other than the repetitious business of tending the animals on the farm morning and night. To me, chores were the essence of animal husbandry, of caring for all the daily needs of farm animals: feed, water and clean, comfortable pens.

The dictionaries (I sought out several) define the word "chores" as some "small, routine task, as a housekeeper or farmer...hard unpleasant task...a small, minor job; incidental piece work...routine duties of a household or farm..." I never thought of chores in that way in the beginning. I knew chores as something mysterious that took Dad away from me, that interrupted our play on the floor. He would put on his barn clothes and go outside and spend a long time before finally returning to the house. I could not imagine where he had gone or what he was doing. Often I stood at the window, my chin on the sill, in those early years, waiting and waiting, watching for him to emerge from the gloom of a winter evening.

Finally, I would see him coming toward the house carrying his lantern in one hand and a pail of foamy milk in the other. I would run to greet him as he entered the kitchen, impatient for him to get out of his boots and winter barn clothes so we could be together again. His thick mittens and jacket carried the heavy reek of barn. They smelled of cows, silage and hay and warm, sweet milk. I looked forward to the time when I could wear clothes that smelled that good.

The time inevitably came when I too put on my denim overalls and barn jacket, boots, cap and mittens and went out to do the chores. But the initiation was gradual. First I observed by following Dad around, trying to keep up with his steps as he watered and fed the horses, pigs, calves and cows. I stood aside in a safe place when he opened the door to the barnyard. The cows, patiently waiting outside, scrambled and shoved their way up the cleated plank ramp through the door to their places in the wooden stanchions. I watched with fascination as they licked up the little mounds of meal at their places. It was for those mounds of meal, as well as for the prospect of being relieved of the burden of milk from their full udders, that the creatures had patiently waited outside the cow barn door.

As some people dress for dinner we dressed for chores — our old, well-worn, comfortable and often smelly clothes.

AN ASSORTMENT OF HEAD DRESS IN WHICH WE FELT COMFORTABLE DOING CHORES

WINTER DRESS

SUMMER DRESS

SEVERAL LAYERS CONSISTING OF UNDERWEAR, SHIRTS, SWEATERS, JACKETS AND OVERALLS

. . . AS LITTLE AS POSSIBLE

TWO OR THREE PAIRS OF COTTON FLANNEL MITTENS

FEET IN 2 PAIR OF HEAVY SOCKS, SHOES and OVERSHOES

7

After the cows' heads were secured in the stanchions, I felt it safe to come close enough to see the milking process. Dad sat down on his strange, one-legged stool beside a cow, clamping a shiny, tinned milk pail between his knees. Then I took the small stool he had made for me, a miniature model of his own, and by propping it against the wall, managed to keep my balance. Thus positioned, I could watch as Dad milked the cow with seemingly little effort. Full, white streams of milk came from the cow's teats.

It looked so easy I asked to try.

"Come on," Dad said, encouraging me to reach across his lap, under the warmth of the cow's great body, and grasp a full teat. I could barely close my fist around it.

"Now," he said, "while holding the teat, close your pointing finger and squeeze the top of the teat against your palm...like this." With his own hand over mine he guided each of my fingers as he continued to speak. "Then close your second finger, and your third and fourth. Close your fist one finger at a time in that order."

"You mean like this?" I asked.

"Right. That's the idea. Now, at the same time you're closing the fist around the teat, pull down gently, like this. See? Now you try it."

I tried with no results. He went through the procedure again and again with great patience until finally I had the squeezing and pulling actions coordinated and managed to produce a few feeble squirts of milk — some of them into the pail. At this point, the cow became nervous and began to fidget and Dad said my first milking lesson was over.

I withdrew to my perch on my one-legged stool against the wall and watched with new appreciation as Dad resumed his expert stroking (much to the relief of the cow) until sweet smelling, foamy milk filled the pail clamped between his knees. He poured a small portion of the milk into a battered pie tin for the meowing cats and emptied the rest into a tall milk can hanging from a spike in a two-by-six timber extending along the wall of the barn.

I would follow these procedures on my own many times over the ensuing years. But before I was old enough to do chores by myself, I helped (and learned) by carrying the kerosene lantern for Dad in the dark winter months as he went about the barn and sheds bearing water, feed and bedding. When my brother, Dean, two years my junior, was old enough, we took turns with the lantern every other night. When we had a hired man we each had a job every night, one of us serving as his lantern carrier too.

About the time my youngest brother, Dan, (ten years younger than I) reached choring age, electricity came to our farm. This event gradually changed the nature of our chores. The moment the power was switched on for the first time, the battered kerosene lanterns were retired to hang, and collect dust and cobwebs, in the shed. Eventually running water, conveyors and a milking machine found a place on our farm. All of them changed many aspects of doing chores. But in the pages of this book we will deal with doing chores in the old way — before our "enlightenment."

Before we were old enough to do chores by ourselves we served our "apprenticeship" by carrying the lantern for Dad. This job had its responsibilities too...

...like turning the flame high enough to make a good light...

...to hold the light so Dad could see...

HEY!

...but not too high!

...and to keep the lantern upright at all times!

Chapter 2
First came the chickens

As we grew older and had graduated from being observers and lantern carriers, we were deemed able to handle the chicken chores by ourselves. Apparently it was thought that there was not too much danger to a little fellow in the chicken yard. Even a very small chore boy (or girl) wasn't apt to be seriously hurt if stepped on by a chicken.

However, there were minor hazards (they seemed major at the time) like getting small fingers in the machinery of the hand-cranked corn sheller, or being attacked by an old cluck or a cranky old rooster with long spurs. But encounters between these chicken-yard bullies and their terrified victims were infrequent, since, in the case of the offending rooster, the attacker was apt to end up on your dinner table. There was a certain satisfaction in the vengence with which the victim could chew on the tough drumstick of his former tormenter.

As for the crotchety old clucks, their punishment wasn't capital even if they were judged guilty. (They were guilty if they puffed up their feathers to appear twice their true size, made a loud squawk and pecked a tender hand or arm as it reached for one of their prized eggs. Actually, these mean old hens seemed quite formidable to a doer of chores. The term "hen pecked" had a very definite meaning to me at an early age.)

The maximum punishment for a guilty hen was to be jailed and fed on corn and water until her broody nature changed and she stopped clucking and was sufficiently rehabilitated to scratch out a living around the farmyard, lay eggs and cackle like a normal, every-day hen.

The lucky clucks, even though guilty, were granted their primitive desires and were put on a nest of about 12 carefully selected fertile eggs and allowed to be full-time setting hens for the next 21 days — until the eggs hatched into chicks, and the old hens, still clucks and still cantankerous, became fulfilled as mothers.

My reference above to the chicken yard was a figure of speech since we had no yard in which the chickens were confined. Only in the winter were they shut up in the chicken house. The rest of the year they were as free as the pigeons to roam the farm wherever they wished. In practice, however, they never ventured far from the farmyard, where, from dawn to sunset, they could be found busily scratching and pecking. They picked up spilled grain, undigested tidbits from animal manure, grass and other greens and, of course, all the insects they could catch.

It was amusing to see a pompous rooster, upon finding a choice morsel, call his harem with a "tut, tut, tut, tut." When two or three of the gullible hens came running, there might be nothing more for them than a pebble. But no matter, the rooster still made a great show of being a good provider. Having the hens at his beck and call seemed to do great things for his ego.

THE CHICKEN CHORES WERE THOSE ONE WAS STARTED ON WHEN VERY YOUNG, BUT NEVER SEEMED TO OUTGROW:

FIRST IT WAS TO THE CORNCRIB TO SHELL THE CORN WITH THE HAND CRANKED SHELLER...
... OR BY HAND

... OR, MAYBE, TO BREAK THE EARS INTO SHORT PIECES.

Tending the chickens was a chore well suited to entertaining small guests. Both girl and boy visitors enjoyed making the rounds of the chicken chores. We went to the corncrib where they helped turn the crank of the corn sheller, then to the oats bin where we could watch the barn swallows fly in and out of the window. (They had a mud nest plastered against a rafter.) Then we scattered the feed on the ground and called "chick, chick' chick" and the feathered bipeds came running from all directions to gobble it up.

THE OATBIN WAS ONE OF THE STOPS IN THE CHICKEN CHORES — CHICKENS LIKED OATS AND THEY WERE AN IMPORTANT SOURCE OF PROTEIN FOR THEM.

CHICK, CHICH, CHICK

WE WONDERED HOW CHICKENS COULD TASTE AND ENJOY THE KERNELS OF GRAIN SINCE THEY HAD NO TEETH TO CHEW BUT SWALLOWED THEM WHOLE.

BUT **ALL** THE TOOTHLESS FOWL SEEMED TO RELISH FEEDING TIME.

13

Probably the best part of chicken chores, and the one that small visitors to the farm enjoyed most, was gathering eggs. It was somewhat like a daily Easter egg hunt.

Most of the eggs were gathered in the hen house where nests had been constructed. But since our chickens roamed free, except during the winter, we had to search out hidden nests in a wide radius from the hen house. This search included the barn, sheds and corncrib. Sometimes we found nests of eggs hidden under a horse manger or under the oat binder or in a board pile in the grove. Sometimes the reclusive hens placed well hidden nests under the great leaves of a burdock plant.

Usually only a few eggs in the hidden nests we found were fresh. If they were smooth and shiny, chances were they were not good. We would carefully shake them next to our ear and if we heard a splash within, those eggs were carefully set aside to be disposed of against a tree or rock away from our living area. We did not want to be subjected to the putrid, sulfurous stench of rotten eggs. Popping these gaseous grenades was great sport, an added incentive for finding a secret nest.

Another aspect of chicken chores that was just as stinking but not nearly as much fun was the disposal of dead chickens in the heat of summer. We tried to do this before we were guided to their putrefying carcasses by the stench. We buried the rotting remains in a hasty, shallow grave in the far corner of the grove.

Sometimes a discovered nest, if it looked to have been there for a time, was left undisturbed (especially if an old cluck was on the nest or nearby) and allowed to hatch.

If the hen was successful in keeping her "stolen" nest a secret and secure from our egg searches — and if the eggs were fertile — there would suddenly appear, one fine summer day, a mother hen with a flock of dusky, downy, peeping chicks clustered about her as she scurried around the farmstead scatching out a living for her new family.

Sometimes these stolen nests hatched out too late in the summer and the chicks were much too young to survive the harsh cold of fall and winter.

The chicken chores "matured," so to speak, as we did. As we got older, we had to share more in the less fun parts of the work.

There was the odious and odiferous task of cleaning out the chicken house periodically; the spraying of roosts, walls and nests for mites; and in winter the spreading of fresh straw under the roosts.

Keeping the nests padded with straw was a yearlong task. The padding guarded against broken or cracked eggs.

Watering the chickens was hard work for little folks. We were spared this job until we could work the hand pump and carry the heavy pails of water to waterers and troughs in the chicken house and at various places around the farmyard. A constant supply of fresh water was mandatory for the production of eggs and the comfort and well being of the chickens, winter and summer. But in the heat of summer we were more conscious of the water needs of all the farm creatures.

I remember the remorse I felt upon finding a drowned chicken in the horse tank where it was trying to get a drink because its watering trough was dry.

PROBABLY THE HARDEST AND THE MESSIEST OF THE CHICKEN CHORES WAS WATERING THEM

THIS INGENIOUS WATERER WITH THE TOP...

..THAT SLIPPED DOWN OVER THE SUPPLY TANK...

...AND ALLOWED THE WATER TO FLOW OUT INTO THE PAN...

...ONLY AS THE CHICKENS DRANK IT DOWN BELOW THE AIR HOLE

CHICKENS, LIKE ALL FOWL, HAD TO TILT THEIR HEADS BACK AND LET THE WATER RUN DOWN.

A WATER FOUNTAIN FOR THE BABY CHICKS CONSISTED OF A SPECIAL ATTACHMENT SCREWED ONTO A FRUIT JAR

IN WINTER WE HAD TO BREAK ICE FROM THE WATERING PAN

Chapter 3
Coping with pigs

Pigs never were my favorite farm animals. Piglets are cute and intelligent little creatures. But they are never cuddly like other farm babies. Baby pigs use their needle-sharp teeth freely from the start. And almost from birth pigs are aggressive and troublesome.

A pig literally follows its nose and its nose gets poked into everything. If the hole a pig's nose gets poked into yields in any way, the rest of the pig will soon follow. Not only do pigs make big holes out of little ones in fences and walls, but they tear up the ground in hog lot and pasture with their tough snouts and muscular necks until it resembles the landscape of a World War I battlefield. I think pigs are the most destructive of all farm animals.

What's more, pigs are, in my experience, dirty slobs. It has been written, I guess by champions of swine, that pigs are by nature clean. Well, I am fairly well qualified to disagree with this startling idea. I have worked very hard, over the years, to give the pigs I have known plenty of opportunities to display their cleanliness. And they have not responded in a way that causes me to change my opinion of their habits of personal hygiene.

No matter how I felt, much of my chore experience dealt with the obnoxious pig. After all, in our corn and hog culture, pigs were an important link between farm and market.

We could start feeding the pigs quite early in our choring careers. However, we were strictly forbidden to enter the hog pen, so we merely hauled what ear corn we could in our little wagon (the task required several loads) and threw it over the fence to the eager pigs, one ear at a time.

This labor-intensive chore took quite a long time. It took even longer when we stopped to observe the fascinating way in which the hungry hogs chomped the kernels off the cobs. It gave my brother and me ideas for eating corn-on-the-cob when roasting ears were in season. (This may have been the basis for Mom's concern that her sons were behaving like pigs at the table.)

When we could handle a full basket of ear corn on one shoulder, the ban on the pig yard was lifted and we had to learn how to deal directly with the hungry, pushy creatures.

I would try, usually unsuccessfully, to sneak into the hog pen, a bushel basket heaped with ear corn on my shoulder, scatter it and hurry back over the fence before the charging, snorting herd inundated me, bushel basket, corn and all.

If, by chance, the acute hearing and olfactory organs of the pigs had not detected my presence in the pig yard, and I was able to get back over the fence without incident, I could practice my hog calling talent. "Pooey, pooey, pig, pig, pig" was usually enough of a call to get them coming in short order. Sometimes I augmented this call by drumming on the bottom of the empty metal basket. I think it was also a sort of celebration of being able to enter and depart the pig yard without being trampled.

Slopping the pigs was another stressful job. Again, it required great stealth to get the gruel-like slop into the troughs without incurring bumps, abrasions or, at least, a bath of the sour mixture. I used to wonder if pigs had a way of absorbing the nourishing slop through their course skin. As much was poured on them, it seemed, as into the trough where they could slurp it up in greedy gulps.

In spite of all the difficulty connected with the job, I liked swilling the pigs. For one thing, I enjoyed mixing the slop, usually consisting of ground oats, linseed meal, skim milk and water. The mixture, about the consistency of a thick milk shake, had a rich, pleasant smell. Sometimes the milk in the mixture would be sour, but even that smelled good. And to see the pigs slick up every last bit from the feed troughs was evidence they thought it delicious.

I would watch the pigs eating with such gusto and wonder if they would lose their appetites if they could know they were eating to their doom. But I now see that knowing the same thing hasn't seemed to curb our own overeating habits.

Chapter 4
Our great and gentle beasts

Tending the horses was probably my favorite year-around chore. I liked the large, gentle beasts, each with its own personality. Old Jim, for instance, was mischievous and as apt to nip at you as not. But he was a perfect gentleman toward my mother. Our old brood mare, Maude, had a gentle, motherly nature. Jack and Jill, a matched pair of blacks, were perennial colts and had always to be handled as juveniles. And Dolly and Daisy, dappled grey roans, were our favorites — steady, quiet and dependable.

Finally, there was Doc, our old, white pony. He was a reluctant playmate, stodgily accompanying us on our excursions around the farm, pulling our cart or carrying us on his bare back. We spent most of our time urging him on. He was said to be part Arabian, but I felt he was more likely part mule.

Of course it wasn't until we were old enough to handle the big beasts that we were permitted to do all the horse chores. But giving them their oats and hay was something we could do when we were quite small. Upon entering the horse barn at feeding time, we were greeted by a chorus of whinnies and nickers, the horse equivalent of banging spoons on the table. Sometimes the horses would gnaw on their mangers in an attempt, apparently, to emphasize their hunger.

Each horse had to be untied and led from his stall to the watering tank. The animals drank deep drafts that went splashing and gurgling down their long throats. I was fascinated by this phenomenon and wondered how giraffes must sound when drinking.

We had to step lively when watering the great beasts to keep our feet from being trampled by their enormous hooves. One of the skills needed for this chore was tying the halter rope. The knot used for this purpose was called, appropriately enough, a halter knot. It was secure enough to hold the powerful horse, yet easy to untie.

We found it best to give the horses their oats before their hay to avoid the danger of pitch fork injuries as they grabbed for it. They could transform a measure of dusty, dry oats into a wet gruel-like mass by mixing it with their saliva in the feed box. Only after slicking up the last bit of slobber-mixed oats did the horses turn to the hay in their manger. Sometimes I would tarry at my task, watching and listening as their great molars ground the hay in their cavernous mouths.

WITH THE EXCEPTION OF FEEDING OATS TO THE HORSES, WHICH WE COULD DO WHEN QUITE SMALL, MOST OF THE **HORSE CHORES** REQUIRED THE WORK OF THOSE OLD ENOUGH TO HANDLE THE LARGE CREATURES

FIRST WE LED EACH HORSE TO THE WATER TANK WHERE IT COULD DRINK ITS FILL

I WAS FASCINATED AT THE SOUND OF THE WATER SPLASHING DOWN THE LONG THROAT.

25

There was adventure in throwing the hay down from the haymow. We climbed into that dusky place, dug the "loose" hay from a great mountain of dusty, sweet-smelling grasses and made a soft, springy pile at the foot of the chute that we could jump into.

The pigeons perched their skimpy nests on high beams overhead, and talked to us (or one another) in their low, throaty tones. Often small kittens with little, pointed tails scampered into dark recesses under the eaves, where they spit and snarled as we reached for them. After several days of this wild behavior, the kittens became tame, their spitting and snarling turning into friendly mewing and purring. Eventually they found their way to the cow barn and the battered pie tin of warm milk.

WE TRIED TO SEE TO IT THAT THE **HAYMOW CHORES** WERE DONE BEFORE DARK — THE LANTERN NOT BEING ALLOWED UP THERE.

THE HAY WAS NOT IN BALES BUT WAS IN ONE LARGE "LOOSE" PILE

HOWEVER, WHEN TRYING TO PULL FORKS FULL FROM THE MOUNTAIN OF PACKED HAY, IT SEEMED ANYTHING BUT LOOSE!

BUT THEN WE HAD WAYS OF RELAXING AFTERWARD →

Before the tractor was widely used on our farm, there was hardly a day when a team of horses was not used. So part of the horse chores was currying and brushing the beasts of burden before putting on their harnesses.

This wasn't very difficult, unless their stall was not clean and they had been lying down. Then, sometimes, there was matted manure to comb out. But generally it meant simply going over their bodies with brush and comb rather quickly. The horses seemed to enjoy it, and Dad insisted on it. He was particular about their appearance in harness.

THE HORSES HAD TO BE CURRIED AND BRUSHED BEFORE THEY WERE HARNESSED — THEY LIKED IT AND WE DIDN'T MIND DOING IT...

CURRYCOMB and BRUSH

...EXCEPT AROUND THOSE BIG HOOVES

Harnessing the horses for work was not an easy task even when we had grown big enough to heft the heavy, complicated assemblage of leather straps, metal buckles, snaps and chains and wooden hames topped with brass balls. The harness hung on two wooden supports behind each horse and had to be lifted from there to the back of the horse so that everything would be in its proper alignment and could be buckled and snapped into place around the horse's body.

But before the harness itself came the collar. It was as important that this part of a work horse's accoutrement fit properly as it is that a shoe fits us properly. The collar was placed around the neck against the shoulder. The hames were attached to it and from them the traces, or tugs, which pulled the load. If the collar was not properly fitted, painful sores could develop, causing the poor beast much pain. Left unattended, the sores from an ill-fitting collar could ruin a good workhorse. We took great care to see that the surface facing the horse was clean and smooth, even to be sure no strands of the hair of the mane were under it.

After the collar was fitted the hames were clamped into place and the girdle, or belly band, was cinched. Finally, the horse's tail was put over the breeching and the crupper was fastened under the tail.

When I first started harnessing the horses (four or six of them), I felt more like taking a vacation than like working them for the next four or five hours in the field.

After the horses were harnessed and before they were led from the barn and hitched to the farm implement to be used that day, we had to remove the halters and put on the bridles.

It was difficult enough to slip off a halter and put on a bridle without allowing the horse to escape. But the procedure was significantly complicated by the metal bit that was to go into the animal's mouth, and to which the horse objected. With practice, you could slip the thumb on each hand into the horse's mouth (behind the teeth) causing him to open his mouth enough to admit the bit, if you moved quickly.

This of course, was messy business, making it necessary to wipe our wet hands on the horse's coat or our own overalls.

THE FINAL PIECE OF HARNESS TO GO ON THE HORSE WAS THE **BRIDLE**

PUTTING ON A HALTER WAS EASY...

...BUT THE BRIDLE HAD THE BIT TO CONTEND WITH... IT HAD TO GO INTO THE HORSE'S MOUTH...

...AND THE HORSE OBJECTED!

The least pleasant part of the horse chores was cleaning their stalls. During the summer this was done daily. But in the winter months the mixture of manure and bedding straw was allowed to accumulate because it served as a sort of carpet and generated heat. When we did clean out this steaming accumulation, the ammonia fumes stung our eyes and our sinuses and permeated our clothes with a distinctly horsey smell.

The best part of cleaning the horse stalls, as of any cleaning job, was putting down a layer of clean straw for the animals to lie in. We sometimes felt the bedding was wasted on the horse, however, for we seldom saw a horse reclining in its straw. A horse can sleep while standing and usually does. In fact, when we found a horse lying down, we immediately suspected it of being sick.

Cows, too, sometimes went to sleep while they were standing, but they apparently were not designed to do so. At any rate, the peaceful, rhythmic sound of milking in our cowbarn, one evening, was suddenly shattered when one of the cows dozed off and crashed to the floor. The sudden jolt awoke her and she scrambled, wide-eyed, to her feet.

Fortunately, she was not being milked at the time, or the milk pail, as well as the person milking her, would have been flattened.

Chapter 5
Cattle call

Our cattle herd included milk cows, beef cows, calves and a bull. The bull served both the milk and the beef cows, since we milked mostly shorthorns or a mixture of shorthorn, Brown Swiss and Holstein.

During the spring and summer, our cattle chores were limited almost entirely to the milking herd. The beef cattle spent the entire period from about April or May to October or November, depending on the weather, in pasture.

If the onset of winter held off long enough, the cattle were turned from pasture into the harvested corn fields where they could glean fallen or missed ears and feed upon the empty husks and dry leaves they seemed to relish. When the snows put an end to foraging in the corn fields, they were shut up in the yards for the winter, and feed had to be carried to them every day.

The main feed for all the cattle, beef as well as dairy, was corn silage. Feeding silage was a heavy task. It began with the daily climb into the silo. This in itself was no small matter, especially for one who seemed not to have enough hands when in high places.

My first trip up into the silo, when I was still in the observer stage of my chore career, was with Dad's reassuring arms on either side of me and his feet on the ladder below mine. Getting from the ladder through the opening into the barrel of the silo was then, and forever after, a maneuver I performed with quickened pulse and white knuckles. I knew a wonderful sense of relief and security once I was inside the barrel and the sweet smelling silage lay beneath me all the way to the ground.

Each time we scooped silage out of the silo and down the long chute, we slightly lowered the chopped corn platform upon which we worked. At the same time we raised an equivalent pile at the bottom of the chute. Perceiving this minute equalizing action was enough to give me some comfort every day. Toward the end of winter, the two columns of silage were close enough together so that I could perform my chores with the nonchalance of a seasoned aerialist.

After throwing a predetermined number of scoops of silage down the chute, we had to carry the same feed, by the basketful, to the cattle. This was not an easy task under the best of conditions (working one's way, with a heavy burden of feed, through shoving, crowding cattle) but in wet, sloppy weather, when the cow yard was deep in mud and manure, the job became extremely difficult, even hazardous. There was always the possibility of being knocked down and trampled into the muck. The prospect kept one alert.

FEEDING THE CATTLE IN WINTER WAS A BIG CHORE.

WE DID NOT HELP WITH IT UNTIL WE WERE BIG ENOUGH TO CLIMB THE SILO LADDER AND CARRY BUSHEL BASKETS OF SILAGE TO THE FEED BUNKS.

THIS PART WAS SCARY

WE COUNTED THE SCOOPS OF SILAGE WE THREW DOWN THE CHUTE

In spite of the heavy work and my daily encounter with the silo's dizzying heights, I liked feeding silage to the cattle. They obviously relished the succulent, sweet and sour chopped corn fodder and I enjoyed its aroma.

There was special satisfaction in carrying the fragrant silage into a clean and freshly bedded cow barn and putting a portion at each cow's place, in readiness for that night's milking session. It was like preparing a banquet hall for some high occasion.

While we generally preferred corn silage as winter feed, there were years when, for one reason or another, we were short of silage and reserved it for the milk cows. In this case, whole corn fodder (including the ears) was fed to the beef herd. Shredded corn fodder (without ears) was fed in addition to silage to all the cattle as a roughage in place of hay.

Feeding the cattle corn fodder was in some ways harder work than feeding silage. If the weather permitted in the fall, we hauled the bundles of dry fodder, with the ears of corn still attached to the stalks, to the farmstead and stacked them near the feeding rack.

I have spoken of the fragrance of silage. Dry corn fodder, especially when quite new, in its sweating or curing stage, also had a rich, ripening smell that was pleasant to the nostrils. The cattle enjoyed this dry feed nearly as much as silage. They searched out and devoured the whole ears before finally cleaning up every leaf and husk, leaving only the heaviest stalks in the bottom of the feed rack.

If the weather prevented gathering the fodder in the fall, we fed the shocks directly from the field, hauling and feeding daily. On many cold, blustery days we dearly regretted not having the fodder stacked near the cow yard.

Hauling corn bundles from shocks in the fields had its adventuresome side for our dog who hunted field mice. Their snug winter homes in the corn were devastated when we tore open the shocks and loaded them onto the wagon. My sympathies were definitely with the little, white bellied creatures trying to escape in terror from the disaster that had befallen them.

The shocks made a perfect winter home for the mice. There was plenty of material for them to shred into fluffy fibers for nests to insulate their tiny, fat bodies from the killing cold. And the ears of corn in each shock assured them of ample food through the long winter.

I did all I could to distract the dog from the terrified little refugees. I wondered where they would go into the snowy winter landscape, and, if they escaped the jaws of the dog, what their fate would be.

We were also kept somewhat in suspense by the possibility that a skunk might be inhabiting one of the corn shocks we were dismantling.

One bonus of hauling corn fodder across snowy fields was the musical, bell-like sound the steel wheels made on the frozen snow. If our toes and fingers were not hurting too much from the cold, we could enjoy the concert the wheels made as we rode deep in the load of corn fodder and the wagon jolted and rocked across the frozen snow-covered fields.

SOMETIMES WE FED THE CATTLE CORN FODDER WHICH WAS ROUGH AND DRY LIKE HAY AND NOT AT ALL SUCCULENT LIKE SILAGE.

WE FED IT FROM A STACK...

...OR HAULED IT DIRECTLY FROM THE SHOCKS IN THE FEILD

...AN INSTRUMENT SUCH AS THIS WAS USED TO CUT THEM LOOSE.

AND WHEN THE SHOCKS WERE FROZEN TO THE GROUND...

Some livestock raisers, before feeding whole bundles of corn fodder, first husked the ears, giving the cattle only the stalks without the corn. This daily task was done by hand. And some farmers shredded the fodder before feeding it.

For several years our farm was included in a corn shredding ring, just as it was in an oats threshing ring. The corn, when ripe, was cut and bound into bundles and made into shocks, so familiar in the autumn fields during those years. Then several neighbors gathered with teams and wagons and hauled the bundles to the shredding machine in the farmyard. This machine separated the ears from the corn stalks and shredded the stalks and leaves into fodder, easily handled with a large, four-tined fork. It was blown into mows or stacks in the barnyard. The ears of corn were put into the corn crib to dry.

Sometimes, when there was a shortage of hay, we even fed shredded corn fodder to the horses. It also made excellent bedding for all the livestock.

Shredding the corn enhanced its ripe fragrance and the sweating period, in stack or mow, intensified it even more, adding a sweet dimension to doing the daily chores in winter. Like hay, the shredded corn made a desirable bed into which we snuggled now and then to take a break for dreaming — either awake or asleep.

SOMETIMES, INSTEAD OF FEEDING THE CATTLE CORN FODDER DIRECTLY FROM THE SHOCK OR FROM A STACK OF BUNDLES, WE FED THEM **SHREDDED CORN FODDER**

THIS WAS FED LIKE HAY FROM THE LOFT IN THE BARN . . .

. . . OR FROM A STACK IN A FEED RACK IN THE CATTLE YARD.

WE LIKED TO PLAY TAG IN AND OUT AND AROUND THESE SHREDDED FODDER STACKS — WHEN THE CATTLE WEREN'T EATING, OF COURSE.

If I were to rate the cleaning of pens and stalls in order of preference, my first choice would be the horse barn. Last on the list would be the pig pens. Cleaning the cow barn would rate second on the scale, a fortunate thing since during the winter months, when the milk cows were kept in the barn overnight, cleaning the cow barn was a daily chore. Still, cleaning the gutter in the cow barn was a job I certainly did not relish.

One discouraging thought that plagued me while I was throwing the heavy mixture of manure, urine and straw, one forkful at a time, onto the steadily growing pile outside the back door of the cow barn was, "Come spring we'll have to pitch this same stuff all over again, one forkful at a time, onto the spreader and haul it into the fields."

We tried to clean out the cow barn in the morning as early as possible after the cows had been turned out for the day. This gave the gutter a chance to dry before the night milking. Even though I found this job distasteful, I enjoyed the good feeling of accomplishment when the task was completed and fresh straw bedding had been spread.

CLEANING THE COW BARN WAS A WINTER CHORE THAT WAS AS EVER-PRESENT AS THAT OF MILKING.

IT WAS A HARD, DISTASTEFUL TASK...

...BUT WHEN THE GUTTER WAS CLEAN AND FRESH STRAW BEDDING WAS SPREAD — THERE WAS SATISFACTION IN A JOB WELL DONE.

Chapter 6
The education of a milker

The milking chores began, in the summer months, with bringing the cows up from our creek pasture. This was my favorite summertime chore. It always offered the potential for adventure.

I would pick up my walking stick from its place by the lower barnyard gate and stride down the lane to the wire pasture gate with a light step. I breathed deeply of the green smell of summer. On either side of the wire-fenced lane were crops: oats, corn or clover. As the season progressed, the plantings grew and matured, and we were able to observe the changes day after day, week after week, from the tender sprouts of early spring to the ripened and harvested crops of early fall. The visible and audible changes brought by the progressions of the season were accompanied by a succession of fragrances from the growing, flowering and ripening vegetation. Even now, if I were to be set down in that place with all my senses erased but smell, I would immediately know the time of year.

Gophers, meadowlarks, red-headed woodpeckers, mourning doves and other creatures, whistled, warbled, chirped and cooed to entertain us as we traversed the cow lane twice daily, seven days a week. And the insects changed with the seasons: first midges, ants, crickets, grasshoppers; then dragonflies, cicadas, katydids; then spiders that rode September breezes on gossamer.

When we passed the barbed wire gate at the end of the lane, we were in a different world. It was a wild, almost primeval place, our slough pasture.

If we were lucky, the cows would be in a far corner of the east pasture. To get to them, we would have a choice of two routes: across the flats, tall with slough grasses and flowers; or along the north rim between the pasture and cropland, where willow, cottonwood, chokecherry and ash trees flourished.

Taking the cowpath through this bit of prairie forest was apt to lead to encounters with the wild creatures that lived among the branches, in the hollow trunks or in burrows among the roots of the trees that grew there. We saw different bird varieties there than in the open fields, and we might encounter squirrels, opossums, raccoons or skunks. If we were fortunate we might glimpse a red fox.

If we chose to take the well worn path across the great flat area we called the bogs, we might see and hear red-winged blackbirds, bobolinks, song sparrows and a marsh hawk protecting its nest.

Then there was the "dark grove," a thick, overgrown tangle of boxelder, ash, black walnut, silver maple, cottonwood and willow. Here the egrets and night herons nested in the canopy overhead.

The creek was always our favorite place. Along it we might scare up a pair of mallard ducks, or sandpipers or a great blue heron. Frogs, turtles and crayfish were also denizens of this watery world. If we thought we could spare the time we forgot the cows for a little while and took a quick dip in the slow moving stream. We were aware of the fish there (minnows, suckers and carp) and also of the annoying blood suckers that seemed to prefer my blood to my brother's.

MILKING CHORES VARIED WITH THE SEASONS, BUT IN SUMMER THEY BEGAN WITH THE SMALL ADVENTURE OF GOING TO THE PASTURE FOR THE COWS

WE EACH HAD A WALKING STICK STASHED AT THE BARNYARD GATE.

SOMETIMES WE SNEAKED IN A COOLING DIP IN THE CREEK BEFORE ROUNDING UP THE COWS

THERE COULD BE ALL SORTS OF ENCOUNTERS WITH WILD CREATURES...

WAYSIDE BANDITS...

AIR ATTACKS...

...AND AMBUSH!

Often more time passed in getting the cows than we had intended, so we usually had to hurry the languid creatures faster than was good for them. We prodded them along, hoping to get to the barn before Dad thought we'd taken too long. Spirts of milk shot from their full udders as they swang back and forth to the rhythm of hurried steps.

The fly season made life miserable for the poor cows. While the pests were generally bothersome, they seemed to be especially vicious on the animals' backs, legs and bellies. To escape them, the cattle often stood belly deep in the creek or in mudholes. This made for extra work in the cowbarn, where we were concerned to keep the milk reasonably clean. I can still smell in my mind the peculiar odor of "crick" mud as we bathed the cows' udders before milking.

Once the cows were in the barn we sprayed them with McKesson's, or some other patented fly spray. We hoped the cows didn't mind the smell of the oil spray as much as we did or they might have preferred the flies. The mist of this pungent mixture, hovering in the hot, stuffy cow barn, seemed to discourage the flies for awhile, giving the cows some temporary relief and us a chance to milk them without so much fidgeting and tail-switching.

Sometimes we would find a lump, about the size of a peanut in the shell, under the skin on a cow's back. It was possible, if pressure was applied in just the right way, to squeeze the lump until a grub popped out and we could destroy it.

SOMETIMES TAKING THE COWS FROM THE PASTURE WAS LIVENED UP A LITTLE

WE TRIED TO KEEP THE COWS CALM WHILE MILKING BY SPRAYING ON McKESSON'S FLY SPRAY

A MUDDY CREEK PASTURE MEANT WASHING OFF THE COWS' UDDERS BEFORE MILKING

After the cows had been brought up from the pasture and had quenched their thirst at the moss-lined stock tank, they gathered in a milling mass outside the cow barn door. They crowded together partly in an attempt to rid themselves of the biting flies and partly to get an advantageous position for the rush into the barn. The rush was governed by a caste system. The shoving and milling reminded each cow of her proper place and encouraged her to respect the rights of those of higher caste.

While the cows were getting their act together, we were making last minute preparations inside the barn. We distributed small portions of ground meal at each cow's place and made sure the stanchions were open. Then the door was thrown back and the thundering herd scurried and shoved up the wooden plank ramp into the barn and found their places in the stanchions. We secured them. Then the fly spray was applied and the udders were washed in readiness for milking.

BEFORE THE COWS WERE PUT INTO THEIR STANCHIONS EACH WAS GIVEN A MEASURE OF GROUND MEAL — SOMETHING TO ENTICE THEM AND HELP PRODUCE MORE MILK.

AND WHEN WE OPENED THE BARN DOOR...

... NO COW HAD BETTER TRY TO GET AHEAD OF THE "BOSS" COW OR SHE WOULD GET PUT IN HER PLACE!

THEN, WITH ALL THOSE FULL UDDERS BEFORE US...

I must have been eight or ten years old before milking was a full-time chore for me. By then, I was an "expert" although never as accomplished as Dad. My mind would wander and my hands would sometimes forget to keep up the steady rhythm necessary for maximum production. Then Dad would remind me and I would tend to business for awhile until my thoughts drifted off again to more interesting things than milking. But as I became more skilled, my hands could work pretty well independent of my thoughts and suddenly I would find the teats to be limp and empty in my hands — the cow having been milked dry.

There were many times, especially after a long day in the fields, making hay or picking corn by hand, when the muscles of my lower arms ached and became weak before the night's milking was done.

Later, when I was in high school, where I was not particularly known for my athletic prowess, I glowed with pride when a classmate, one day, grabbed my forearm and exclaimed over its muscularity. Suddenly I could appreciate the milking chore as having some beneficial side effects. Looking back on those times now, I see many benefits that I was not aware of at the time.

Sometimes, if we weren't too weary from a long, hard day, we discussed a wide range of topics. Often the subjects were light and entertaining and cause for hearty laughter that broke the tedium of milking. But sometimes our discussions dealt with the mysteries of the universe and of life and death.

It was at the warm side of a cow that I received answers to my questions concerning the facts of life. During milking sessions my brothers and I got straight answers to the questions and concerns of growing boys. In those days it seemed that the very word "sex" was dirty. But the facts were everywhere around us to observe and puzzle over in the farm animals, and in our feelings as we developed toward adulthood. Dad's down to earth answers helped to straighten out the confusing signals that were assaulting our senses, from within as well as from without. And it was usually in these milking session discussions that we were counseled and given answers to our questions — answers that made sense when coupled with our observations around the farm.

Earlier I mentioned the rhythm in milking. Sometimes we would break into song or whistling while milking. Our repertoire consisted of old, well known (and well worn) favorites: "Let Me Call You Sweetheart," "Down by the Old Mill Stream," "Bicycle Built for Two," "The Missouri Waltz," "Yankee Doodle," "I've Been Working on the Railroad," "Redwing," "Every Little Movement," and others. Later, after we had our battery powered Atwater Kent radio, we added pieces like "Springtime in the Rockies," "Tiptoe Through the Tulips," "Red River Valley," and "Home on the Range" to our cowbarn concerts.

Sometimes the enormity of the chore of milking was overwhelming

One had to know how to get ONE SQUIRT AT A TIME:

THE TEAT WAS GRASPED AT THE TOP BETWEEN THUMB AND FOREFINGER

THEN WITH A GENTLE DOWNWARD TUG...

...THE FIST WAS GRADUALLY CLOSED...

...UNTIL THE TEAT WAS SQUEEZED EMPTY OF MILK.

THIS MOTION WAS REPEATED UNTIL THE UDDER WAS EMPTY AND/OR THE PAIL WAS FULL

THEN, ON TO THE NEXT COW FOR A REPEAT PERFORMANCE

Some of the songs were rhythmically better suited to milking than others. When necessary, we altered a rhythm to make a song fit for milking.

We felt the cows liked our music, since they seemed generally quieter during our concerts. However, there were times, if we were concentrating more on the performance of the music than on the business at hand, when we might be rudely interrupted by a critter we considered insensitive to the finer things in life. But the truth probably was that we ourselves were being insensitive — to the basic things in a cow's life, such as chapped or cut teats.

Sometimes we inadvertently entertained guests in our cow barn — we certainly didn't plan it that way. Usually this situation came about because we had been late in coming in from the field.

Relatives or friends might drop in to visit and find us not in the house or on the front porch enjoying a summer evening, but instead in the cow barn, sweaty and smelly, laboring between hot, panting cows whose tails were flailing their sides (and us) in a futile attempt to drive off biting flies.

Usually these cow barn callers were male but occasionally they would include women or girls in clean, starched dresses. At such times, I felt embarassed by my dirty, smelly role. This was especially true if the cow I was milking decided to relieve herself and a stream of urine splashed into the gutter or several pounds of feces plopped to the floor. About this time our female guests, in their dainty attire, would excuse themselves, make a hasty exit, and I would bury my attentions in the business of milking, silently cursing the uncouth beasts with which I was forced to have such close associations.

When the cows were first turned out to pasture in the spring, there was a time when their digestive tracts were not yet accustomed to the change from dry winter fare to fresh green grass and their bowels were extremely loose. Once one of our visitors left the barn with an olive green stain on his white shirt. He had carelessly stood behind a cow, so afflicted, when she coughed.

I suppose milking cows by hand, and the attending duties, included much for teaching humility — one had literally to lower one's self below the cow's level to perform the task. Our close association with cows was an object lesson in our interdependent relationship with creatures other than those of our own species.

Milking time brought not only the cows and their milkers (and flies and occasionally visitors) to the barn, but also the barn cats, morning and night, for their doled-out portion of the warm, sweet lactic fluid. They would sit, paws tucked in, tails wrapped around themselves, quietly waiting until one of us finished with a cow. As we stood up, the pail of milk in one hand and the stool in the other, they sprang to life, converging around our feet, and, in a chorus of mewing, begged for milk to be poured into their battered pie tin.

When one of the cows freshened, there was the added chore of breaking the new calf to drink from a pail. The calf would be allowed to nurse his mother for a few days, as nature intended, and then it was time to wean the calf.

The poor little creature was programmed to suck on a teat, so we had to trick him by letting him suck one of our milk-dipped fingers. When he was vigorously sucking the finger we lowered it and his muzzle into the warm fresh milk. As he continued to suck, we carefully slipped the finger out of his mouth in hopes he would carry on and thus learn to get milk from the pail without aid of the finger.

Eventually, after much splashing, when both calf and trainer were drenched and sticky with warm, sweet milk, the little creature would finally get the hang of it.

I'm sure it was a harrowing experience for the calf — he must have thought we were trying to drown him when we pushed his head down into the bucket of milk almost up to his eyes.

Sometimes the inventiveness of our species causes us to turn our skills into methods of getting the best of our fellow beings. So it was with the pastoral skill of milking. At times we used it as a weapon against man and beast. We would turn a cow's teat at an angle, aiming it at an unsuspecting victim and shoot a stream of warm milk into an ear. This usually brought an immediate response of some kind. At least it was not a lethal weapon.

THERE WERE SOME "SPIN OFF" CHORES CONNECTED WITH MILKING...

...LIKE GIVING WARM MILK TO THE DEMANDING CATS

... AND BREAKING THE NEW CALF TO DRINK FROM A PAIL

AND THEN THERE WAS FUN TOO...

A WELL-AIMED SQUIRT OF MILK COULD...

PLEASE A CAT...

OR MAKE SOMEONE ANGRY

When the milking was finally done, there was still the separating to do.

Our separator was powered by a hand crank. If we thought the chore of milking had taken the last bit of our energy, we knew we had better recharge our resources between barn and milkhouse. The crank turned with great resistance and it took several turns of accelerating speed to get the heavy bowl spinning fast enough to separate the cream from the whole milk. This speed had to be maintained until all of the milk had been run through the separator. When we were tired this took forever.

We could stop cranking when the last of the milk had been run through the separator. The spinning bowl was allowed slowly to decelerate to a stop. In the meantime, the container in which the cream had been collected was covered and suspended by a strap in the water in the cooling tank, where it was kept for a few hours until the animal heat had gone out of it. Later, the cooled cream from this container was added to the daily collection in the cream can, also in the cooling tank, where it was half submerged in the cold water.

This can of cream was taken to the creamery twice a week.

PART OF THE MILKING CHORES, COMING IMMEDIATELY AFTER MILKING ITSELF WAS **SEPARATING**.

STRAINER

MILK SUPPLY TANK

SINCE WE HAD NO ELECTRICITY THE SEPARATOR WAS HAND POWERED...

...ALMOST 60 TURNS PER MINUTE— EVEN WHEN WE WERE TIRED

WHERE THE MILK AND CREAM ARE SEPARATED

CREAM

SKIM MILK

THEN THE LID WAS PUT ON THE CREAM CAN AND THE CAN PUT IN THE COOLING TANK.

After the separating there was yet more to do. While the separated or skimmed milk was still warm, some of it was taken to the calf barn and fed to calves that had mastered the art of drinking from a pail. Even though these calves had been pail-trained, feeding them was still an exciting and messy task. Each wanted to be first, and when they had drunk their portion they wanted more, so there was a lot of shoving and splashing.

Feeding them the milk seemed to stimulate their sucking instinct and they would grab onto each other's ears, dewlaps or any other appendage they could get hold of, and suck vigorously until we were able to distract their attention with oats in their feed trough.

The calves having been fed, the rest of the skimmed milk, with its head of foam, was dumped into the swill barrel where it was mixed with ground meal and water and fed to the pigs.

Washing out the milk pails with cold water (in summer) and a disinfectant was the very last of our milking chores, so we didn't mind it much. It was a noisy and splashy job, with the clatter of tin pails on the cement floor and quantities of water dashing about.

When washed, the pails were hung to drain and dry on racks in readiness for the next milking session, which came all too soon, day after day after day.

The conglomeration of odors (cow, hay, silage, ground meal, milk, fly spray) associated with milking combines to make a single, distinctive smell. To this day I draw a deep breath of appreciation as I pass by a barn where cows are milked. It conjures up many memories.

RIGHT ATER SEPARATING, WHILE THE SKIM MILK WAS STILL WARM, **WE FED THE CALVES** THAT WERE TRAINED TO DRINK FROM THE BUCKET

THE REST OF THE SKIM MILK WENT INTO THE **SWILL BARREL** FOR THE PIGS

THEN, FINALLY THERE WAS THE **WASH-UP.**

Chapter 7
Housecleaning and other calamities

Our family farm was short staffed. My brothers and I had no sisters. I think my parents, who had siblings of the opposite sex, missed having girls. But my brothers and I were blissfully unaware of the incompleteness of our family circle and thought our lives were just about perfect — until it came time to do household chores. Then we wished for two or three sturdy sisters to help Mom.

In our simple world, the division of labor decreed that girls did housework and boys worked outside. It was very comforting to know your place, if you were content in it. But I could not imagine how anyone could be happily resigned to household chores, unless, of course, one were made that way, as girls obviously were — just as they were made to have babies. So it was often with a feeling of martyrdom that my brothers and I did chores that would, in our view, naturally have fallen to a sister.

I don't know where we got these sexist notions. Perhaps we brought them home from school, as we did chicken pox, measles and stomach flu. We did not learn them by example at home, for many times we saw Dad in the kitchen cooking, washing dishes, doing laundry. Sometimes his help was necessary, and sometimes he pitched in just to work with Mom, at the laundry, in particular.

Regardless of our feelings, my brothers and I did help with household chores — partly, in fairness to our better nature, out of wanting to help Mom, and partly by coercion.

The water carrying chores were quite acceptable to our labor code because they required manly strength. Except for emptying the chamber pots. This I thought a very degrading job. I would rather clean a cowbarn anytime than empty the pots. If I ever thought of running away, from home, it was when it came my turn for that loathsome task.

SINCE WE DIDN'T GROW GIRLS ON OUR FARM, **HELP** WITH THE **HOUSEHOLD CHORES** FELL TO US— MY BROTHERS AND ME.

WE CARRIED WATER **INTO** THE HOUSE FOR DRINKING, COOKING, BATHING, AND LAUNDRY.

THEN WE CARRIED **OUT** THE WASTE...

DISHWATER

KITCHEN SWILL

BATH AND/OR WASHWATER

THIS IS AWFUL

AND THE MOST HUMILIATING OF ALL —THE SLOP JARS OR CHAMBER POTS

A BOOK OF CHORES

In the Army, when I was assigned to K.P. duty as punishment for some minor infraction, I was being hit where it really hurt. For this meant washing mountains of dishes, greasy pots and pans, and scrubbing acres of floors.

Of course, doing kitchen work at home was nothing like toiling in that Army kitchen. I liked being in our kitchen at home, for one thing. After all, that's where we usually found Mom; and the cookie jar was there. Still, that desirable, homey place seemed a great deal different when viewed through the steam over a dishpan.

Through my kitchen experience I think I might have gained insight into Mom's sometimes weary lack of enthusiasm when her thundering herd came charging into the kitchen at mealtime, hungry for the food she had provided but not fully appreciative of all that went into its preparation. I hope she was able to get some satisfaction in seeing us wolf down the pan-fried steak, mashed potatoes and gravy, fresh-from-the-oven buns and rhubarb pie she had made, and then ask for more.

Sometimes I dried the dishes while Mom washed. This I didn't mind. We talked of interesting things then. And there was the comfort of knowing that Mom was in charge, relieving me of the burden of thinking or being responsible. When my brother and I did the dishes by ourselves, we both tried to boss but neither wanted any responsibility. There were so many details to tend, like watching to see that the water didn't get greasy and that the glasses weren't streaked.

There weren't the pleasant smelling dish detergents of today (at least not at our house). We used a hunk of yellow homemade lye soap. It got the dishes clean but made our hands red and sore.

I was fond of eating fried chicken, gravy and all those delicious, messy things. But washing up the pots and pans after such a meal was enough to make me want to change my eating habits. Slicking up the last spoonful of gravy from your plate with a piece of bread was one thing, but washing gravy off a plate in the dishpan was quite another.

Often when my brother and I did the dishes, we had to wipe up the kitchen floor too. Next time, we always vowed, we would be less sloppy.

Our kitchen duties did not include cooking. Of course we could make ourselves peanut butter and jelly sandwiches, serve ourselves a dish of Post Toasties, or stir up a cool drink of McNess's fruit nectar and cold water from the well. But anything involving cooking food on the range was something none of us, especially Mom, wanted. My one or two attempts at frying an egg produced a concoction that was not only hard but nearly brittle. There were no cake mixes then, so I wouldn't have dreamed of getting involved in the mysterious and wonderful magic of making a cake. Mom was truly our provider and the master of her kitchen.

In the beginning of time, when the order of things was being established, it was decreed that Monday was for washing clothes and Tuesday was for ironing them. Seldom was this order broken at our house, unless the weather or some other act of God interferred; when it was, the whole week was thrown off schedule.

During school vacations my brothers and I were likely to be very much involved in the washing chores — at least to the extent of carrying water to the boiler and rinse tubs and emptying the dirty water when the washing was done. Often we were also drafted to furnish the power on the hand operated, wooden washing machine and to turn the crank on the clothes wringer when our garments were transferred from wash to rinse and from rinse water to clothes basket.

Mom was in charge and took care of such technical details as seeing that the clothes were separated and washed in proper order. The white things went in first, after being cooked in the clothes boiler. Last to be run through the wash were the overalls and throw-rugs. By that time, the wash water was almost thick and had a stinky, soapy smell, derived partly from the homemade laundry soap we used.

Mom hung the clothes on the line to dry. She alone knew how to do it so the clothes would dry properly, and I never asked to learn. However I did occasionally take the clothes off the line when they had dried (hurriedly, at times, before an approaching rain storm). The smell of clean, fresh, sun-dried clothes piled high in a wooden apple basket is another fragrance I have come to appreciate.

After the last load — overalls, throw-rugs, scrub rags, etc. — had been run through the wash, the water was emptied (in the summer on the flower beds), and the tubs were rinsed and put away until next week.

I did not mind wash day so much in the summer (though it did use up valuable time), when we worked in the shed or in the cool grass under the evergreen. But during the cold months, when our kitchen was the laundry, I hated it. Steam poured from the clothes boiler on the kitchen stove and from the washer; rinse tubs and piles of dirty clothes crowded the room; it wasn't a very pleasant place to be.

We frequently missed the actual washing; Mondays usually found us in school. But often we came home to find temporary clothes lines strung in the kitchen, dining room and living room, because the weather wasn't suitable for drying outside.

To this day the smell of boiled cabbage reminds me of wash day. It seemed that boiled clothes and boiled cabbage went together — though, thankfully, not in the same vessel.

Tuesday's ironing did not involve me directly. Mom reserved that toilsome task for herself. I can still see her taking up a hot flat iron with the lifter from the top of the kitchen range, testing it with a wet finger and then ironing the dampened shirt she had taken from a basket in which other to-be-ironed garments rested in dampened rolls. She worked on a creaking old ironing board. When the iron began to cool, after several passes over a dampened, steaming garment, she returned it to the stovetop, and took another that was hot. This went on and on for hours at a time. What a great thing no-iron fabrics are!

When electricity finally came to our farm, an electric iron was the first appliance Mom bought.

Washing the separator was similar to washing the dishes. Maybe that is why Mom did the irksome chore most of the time. Of the many tasks she had to do, I think washing the separator was the one she disliked the most. It is the only one about which I can ever remember her complaining.

Sometimes the job fell to us boys, so it was easy for me to understand her aversion to it. It was a tedious chore involving many complicated parts (about 50) with tinned surfaces and hard-to-get-at areas. The most tedious and time consuming parts were the forty-some thin metal disks that made up the core of the bowl in which the separating process took place. These cone-shaped disks were numbered and had to be carefully washed, rinsed and strung, one at a time, in sequential order on the drying rack.

Residue and impurities in the milk collected on the inside surface of the bowl and formed a dirty grey layer of cheesy material that the dogs relished.

The only pleasant thing about washing the separator in the summer was that it was a cool job. We used cold water with a disinfectant.

After the parts were all cleaned, they were stacked in the supply tank and covered with a clean dish towel, ready to be assembled and put into place on the separator chasis at milking time.

My brothers and I didn't take much part in butter churning. By the time we were old enough to be of help, our cream was being hauled to the creamery where it was commercially churned into butter.

However I do remember the home process and the experience of cranking the wooden barrel churn for what seemed like ages before the butter finally formed. The moment of its forming was an exciting event. Then the churn was opened, the buttermilk was drained off and the golden colored butter was paddled into a large wooden bowl where it was salted and the remaining buttermilk was worked out of it. After that, the fresh butter was made into one-pound patties and wrapped in waxed paper to be taken to town and traded for groceries.

The cultured commercial buttermilk sold at the dairy departments of today's supermarkets is but a poor substitute for the real stuff poured out of a wooden butter churn. This sour, thin, milky liquid, with little flecks of butter floating in it, was a zesty, refreshingly cool drink, especially good for washing down homemade doughnuts.

Anything having to do with cleaning was repugnant to me. However, as in cleaning the cow barn or our enclosed back porch, there was a certain satisfaction in seeing the change one could make by a little bit of diligent effort.

The porch (the shanty) was, in practice, the main entrance to our house. Our front door, avoided by everyone except strangers not acquainted with rural ways, was seldom used. So Mom was very conscious of the appearance it presented to visitors.

It was a much used place. The screen door usually banged a couple hundred times a day during the summer months when we were home all day long. It was also a repository for all sorts of things attendant to our busy farm life. It was where we left our boots, egg-gathering basket, cob pail, coal bucket and swill pail (full or just emptied); it was where we hung the lanterns when not in use, kept the kerosene can, stacked the stove wood, hung our straw hats, barn caps and jackets; it was where the dogs liked to loiter, the flies to congregate and the barn cats (those we had foolishly tamed) to wait for a kitchen handout. It was where the "valuables" we boys found were left for further disposition: pretty stones, empty turtle shells, bird eggs, pheasant feathers. And since this was the last stop (Mom hoped) for dirt, there was an overworked gunny sack door mat on which we wiped our feet. Cleaning the back porch and keeping it presentable was not a simple task.

Keeping the privy clean did not have the same priority as maintaining a tidy back porch; after all, not many visitors to the farm (thank goodness) had occasion to use it. Still, since it was our only "facility," we felt (Mom felt) it must be kept reasonably presentable.

But no amount of scrubbing the seats and floor boards with strong lye water, of sprinkling lime in the abominable pit, of tidying up the reading material, could very much change the atmosphere of that necessary but loathsome place. We did not know of air fresheners at that time, and I doubt, in any case, that they would have been very effective.

I didn't much mind carrying in wood, coal and corn cobs for the stoves. After all, the chore produced tangible results. Fuel for the living room stove helped to make cozy evenings, and fuel for the kitchen range translated into all the wonderfully delicious meals that Mom coaxed from that old iron and nickle plated marvel.

There were negative aspects to this chore, however. For one thing, the job was never-ending. And the need for more fuel ("right now") always seemed to come at inopportune times when we were busy enjoying ourselves. There was the realization, too, that except for the smoke particles and unburned gasses that went up the chimney and into the atmosphere, and except for the energy that warmed our rooms and cooked our food, we had to carry out in the form of ashes and clinkers all that was left of the corn cobs, chunks of wood and lumps of coal we had carried in. This seemed a double burden.

Dad and Grandpa usually split the chunks of willow, ash, maple, boxelder and wild cherry wood into smaller pieces to be used in the cook stove. But we boys were expected to carry them to the wood box and to the back porch where they were stacked out of rain and snow. We could, and often did, make play of this that helped us to forget it was work. However, there were times when it took a great deal of imagination to hide the reality of the work from our tired muscles.

Hauling buckets full of corn cobs for the stove was a comparatively easy and pleasant task when we could scoop them from the cob pile in the shed. But when that supply was gone, we had to select clean, dry cobs from the hog lot where the pigs were fed. This unpleasant chore meant working among the always-hungry creatures, who thought we had brought them something to eat and would not leave us alone.

Because we tried to make the most of everything we had on the farm, some of the ashes and clinkers carried from our stoves were put to several uses.

We often sprinkled the wood ashes on the garden ground in the winter, for its potash. Wood ashes were also used, sometimes, in making homemade lye for soap.

The cindery ash from a coal fire was sometimes used in place of sand on icy spots around the farmyard in winter. The drawback in this was that the ashes occasionally got tracked back into the house.

And sometimes we would dump a pan of ashes into the hog lot where the pigs licked up bits of it, apparently to satisfy their potassium needs. It was fun to hear them crunch an occasional piece of clinker as we eat peanut brittle candy.

Since we grew up on a farm without electricity, we had chores that those who were not so disadvantaged knew nothing about.

When daylight was gone, for example, we depended upon the lighted wick of a kerosene lamp to help push back the darkness. Keeping these lamps filled, the wicks trimmed and the chimneys cleaned was an ever-present task that often fell to my brothers and me.

It was not easy to pour kerosene into a lamp without running it over. When we spilled, we were plagued by the pervasive, offensive odor of that oily liquid for some time, in our mittens, on our hands or about the lighted lamp on the table before us.

The woven cotton wick, designed to absorb the oil by capillary action and to burn with a steady, clean flame, sometimes developed carbon irregularities. Then the flame would flare up in a smoky point that smudged the glass chimney. So it was necessary to keep the burned edge of the wick trimmed symetrically.

SINCE WE DID NOT HAVE ELECTRICITY THERE WAS THE DAILY CHORE OF **TENDING THE OIL LAMPS**

KEROSENE

THEY HAD TO BE **FILLED**...

...THE **WICKS TRIMMED**

...AND THE **CHIMNEYS WASHED** AND **POLISHED**

There were two household chores I especially hated — one was spring housecleaning and the other was fall housecleaning. A holiday-like frenzy went into this institutionalized, semi-annual ritual of our culture. I would have liked to have had nothing to do with it.

But it was next to impossible to escape housecleaning, even if one was so fortunate as not to get involved in the work of it. If one had been bedridden, I think, one could still not have escaped its widespread disruptions. The whole house was turned upside down and inside out, and swept, dusted and scrubbed until nothing seemed the same. You felt like you'd moved into a strange house.

Thanks to electricity and the way it has changed our living habits (the vacuum cleaner has arrived, for instance) the horrible agony of spring and fall housecleaning has (I hope) become extinct.

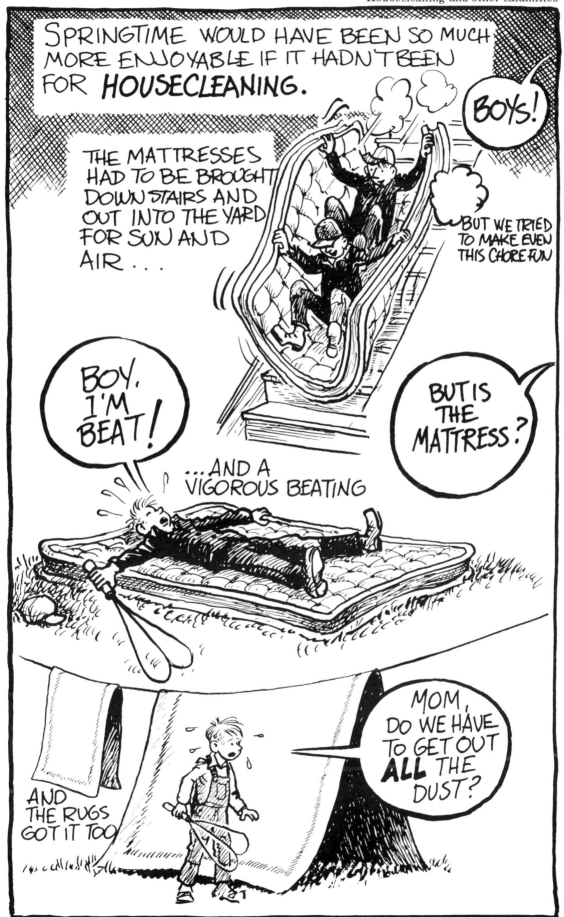

Chapter 8
Chores on ice

Chores in the winter were apt to take a good share of the day. Not only was there the basic work of feeding and watering the livestock morning and night, but the pens and stalls had to be cleaned and fresh straw and bedding had to be spread. If the pens being bedded were not near the straw supply, the job required a team and wagon. That meant first getting the horses harnessed and hitched and then unhitched and unharnessed afterward. But even the basic chores of feeding, and especially watering, became more complicated and time-consuming in freezing weather.

During a long spell of sub-zero cold, the difficulty in watering the livestock intensified. We had no electricity and no pressurized water system. The pump was powered by a gasoline engine that sometimes didn't want to start. Then it took a lot of cranking and priming before it coughed and caught and we heard its healthy "pop, pop, poppety pop."

Our plumbing consisted of a single underground pipe from the well to the stock tank near the barn. The water in this pipe would sometimes freeze during a long period of intense cold. If a corn cob torch on the end of a wire didn't thaw it out in the well pit, it was evident the pipe was frozen underground out of reach of our torch. When that happened, there was little chance of water flowing through it again until spring when the frost went out of the ground.

On the rare occasions when the underground water pipe between the well and the stock tank froze, there was no way it could be thawed. So it was necessary to set up a makeshift aqueduct to carry the water overland, until the ground thawed in its own time. This arrangement was a nuisance. Since it was an obstruction to barnyard traffic, it had to be set up and taken down each time it was used.

Much of wintertime choring involved watering the livestock. Except for the cows and horses, which drank directly from the stock tank, drinking water for the rest of the livestock had to be carried in heavy, dripping pails and poured into troughs, tubs and waterers. This was a cold, wet, icy business. Our lower pant legs and boots became encased in ice, and often our layered mittens also became wet and frozen, adding to the discomfort.

Some of the waterers had kerosene lamps meant to prevent them from freezing. Keeping these lamps filled and lit and the water in the liquid state was an ongoing battle.

SOMETIMES, DURING A PROLONGED PERIOD OF SUB ZERO COLD, OUR ONLY UNDERGROUND WATER PIPE (FROM THE WELL TO THE STOCK TANK) WOULD FREEZE...

...WE HAD TO RIG UP A TEMPORARY AQUEDUCT.

THIS WAS OUR ONLY **RUNNING** WATER...

...THE REST OF IT WAS **WALKED** TO QUENCH THE THIRST OF HOGS, CHICKENS CALVES, TURKEYS AND SHEEP.

KEEPING THE KEROSENE HEAT LAMP GOING UNDER THE HOG WATERER WAS A CONSTANT VIGIL DURING FREEZING WEATHER

The heater in our stock tank was intended to keep the water from freezing. But it was hard to keep it fueled with corn cobs and/or coal, burning all the time, so there was often the added chore of breaking the ice and removing the great, dripping chunks from the tank before the livestock could drink. (This ice pile by the tank supplied us when we wanted to make ice cream.)

The abundance of wind-driven snow compounded the hardships caused by the sub-zero cold. It piled into huge drifts around the farmyard and in the groves. It blocked the lanes and driveways and made gates and doorways unusable. Every cold wind during that time meant more drifting snow and more paths to be dug and re-dug. We opened up passages across the obliterated landscape of our farmyard, through which to carry feed and bedding from grain bins and fodder stacks to our cold, hungry animals. This was done with scoop shovels, bent backs and aching muscles.

Through all of this we suffered twice — once for ourselves and once for our animals.

A BOOK OF CHORES

After I was old enough to carry the responsibility of all of the chores, there were times when I found the work pleasant and satisfying. These were the times when the temperature was not far below freezing but still cold enough to keep the barnyards from being sloppy; when the hay and straw and grain and ground meal were near at hand; when the livestock were secure in snug, dry pens and stalls; and the watering facilities were in good working order. Then I enjoyed winter chores.

There was the satisfaction of making the final round of inspection at night. I held the lantern high so I could see into the darkened corners of the barn. It was comforting to see the horses, blinking their eyes in the sudden light, quietly finishing the hay in their mangers; the calves in the deep straw in their pen, slicking up the last bit of ground corn in their feed bunks; the cows stopping momentarily from chewing their cuds, to stare wide-eyed at my intrusion; and our old dog, Scamp, curled up in his nest of hay, giving me a few thumps of his tail as a "good night" before I closed the barn door.

My boots crunched in the frozen snow as I crossed the farmyard in the circle of light from the lantern that I carried. With the dark, snug barn behind me and the warm glow from the kitchen window ahead, I felt the urge to call out, "Chores are done and all's well!"

94